pres

On Blueberry Hill

by

Sebastian Barry

First performed at the Pavilion Theatre,
Dún Laoghaire, as part of the Dublin Theatre Festival,
27 September to 8 October and at Centre Culturel
Irlandais 11 to 12 October, 2017

Cast

CHRISTY Niall Buggy
PJ David Ganly

with the voice of Ronan Collins *as himself*

Production Team

Directed by Jim Culleton
Set and Costume Design by Sabine Dargent
Lighting Design by Mark Galione
Sound Design by Denis Clohessy
Production Manager Stephen Bourke
Stage Managers Steph Ryan and Tara Doolan
Dramaturg Gavin Kostick
Assistant Director Jeda de Brí
Design Assistant John Galvin
Produced by Eva Scanlan
Graphic Designer Publicis Dublin
PR Sinead O'Doherty at Gerry Lundberg PR
Marketing Chandrika Narayanan-Mohan
Stills Photographer Patrick Redmond

*The production runs for approximately 110 minutes,
with no interval.*

Biographies

Sebastian Barry

was born in Dublin in 1955. His novels and plays have won, among other awards, the Kerry Group Irish Fiction Prize, the Costa Book of the Year award, the Irish Book Awards Best Novel, the Independent Booksellers Prize and the James Tait Black Memorial Prize. He also had two consecutive novels, *A Long Long Way* (2005) and *The Secret Scripture* (2008), shortlisted for the Man Booker Prize. He lives in Wicklow with his wife and three children.

Jim Culleton

is the artistic director of Fishamble: The New Play Company. For Fishamble, he has directed productions which have won Olivier, Stage, Fringe First, Herald Angel, Argus Angel, 1st Irish, Adelaide Fringe and Irish Times Theatre awards, on tour throughout Ireland, UK, Europe, Australia, New Zealand and the US. Current and recent productions for Fishamble include *Maz and Bricks* by Eva O'Connor, *Inside the GPO* by Colin Murphy (staged in the GPO for Easter 2016), *Invitation to a Journey* (with David Bolger, in co-production with CoisCeim, Crash Ensemble and GIAF), *Mainstream* by Rosaleen McDonagh (project co-production), *Tiny Plays for Ireland and America* (Kennedy Center, Washington DC, and Irish Arts Center, New York, for *Ireland 100*), *Spinning* by Deirdre Kinahan (Dublin Theatre Festival), *Little Thing, Big Thing* by Donal O'Kelly (touring in Ireland, UK, Europe, US, Australia), and the multi award-winning *Forgotten, Silent* and *Underneath* by Pat Kinevane (touring to over 60 Irish venues and in 17 other countries). Jim previously directed the multi award-winning *The Pride of Parnell Street*, also by Sebastian Barry, for Fishamble. He has also directed for the Abbey Theatre, Woodpecker/the Gaiety, 7:84 (Scotland), Project Arts Centre, Amharclann de hIde, Tinderbox, The Passion Machine, The Ark, Second Age, RTE Radio 1, The Belgrade, TNL Canada, Dundee Rep Ensemble, Draíocht, Barnstorm, TCD School of Drama, Origin (New York), Vessel (Australia), Little Museum of Dublin, Symphony Space Broadway and Irish Arts Center (New York) and RTE lyric fm. Jim has taught for NYU, NUIM, GSA, Notre Dame, Uversity, TCD and UCD.

Niall Buggy

has worked extensively on the stage and screen in Ireland, the UK and the US. Some of his better known roles include: the title role in Brian Friel's *Uncle Vanya*, for which he won Best Actor at The Irish Times Theatre Awards and for his role as Casimir in *Aristocrats* for which he won the Time Out Award, Obie Award in New York, Drama Desk Award and a Clarence Derwent Award. He also received the Olivier Award for Best Comedy Performance in *Dead Funny*. His performance in *Juno and the Paycock* won him Best Actor in the TMA Awards. Most recent theatre includes: *You Never Can Tell* (The Abbey Theatre), *St. Joan* (Donmar Theatre, London), *The Importance of Being Earnest* (Harold Pinter Theatre), *Translations* (Sheffield Crucible), *The Hanging Gardens* (Abbey Theatre) and *A Whistle in the Dark* with the Druid/Murphy season. Film appearances include: *Mr. Turner*/Mike Leigh, *Mamma Mia*, *Casanova*, *The Butcher Boy*, *Alien 3* and *The Playboys*. Television credits include: *My Mother and Other Strangers* (BBC), *Jack Taylor* (Taylor Made Films), *Inspector Lewis*, *Dalziel and Pascoe*, *Father Ted*, *The Bill* and *The Professionals*.

David Ganly

trained at the Samuel Beckett Centre, Trinity College. Theatre includes: Valene in *Lonesome West* at the Tron Theatre, Glasgow, Fluther in *The Plough and the Stars* at the Abbey Theatre Dublin and US and Irish tours, Seamus in *Shadow of a Gunman* at Abbey Theatre, Dublin, and the Lyric Theatre, Belfast, Burbage in *Shakespeare in Love* at Noël Coward Theatre, Mac the Knife in *Threepenny Opera* at Gate Theatre, Dublin, Kent in *King Lear*, Theatre Royal Bath, Lumpy in *Drum Belly* at the Abbey Theatre, Dublin, Banquo in *Macbeth* at the Sheffield Crucible, Lennie in *Of Mice and Men* at the Watermill, Newbury, The Cowardly Lion in *The Wizard of Oz* at the London Palladium, Pato in *Beauty Queen of Leenane* at the Young Vic (Offie nomination for Best Actor), Amos in *Chicago* at the Cambridge Theatre London, Brendan in *The Weir* at the Gate Theatre, Dublin, Peter Hall's production of *Uncle Vanya*, *The Cavalcaders* at the Abbey Theatre Dublin, Brian Friel's *Translations* for the National Theatre, *Hamlet* for the Theatre Royal Northampton, *Observe the Sons of Ulster Marching towards the Somme* for the Abbey Theatre, Dublin. He created the role of Father Welsh in Martin McDonagh's *The Lonesome West*, part of *The Leenane Trilogy* directed by Garry Hynes at the Druid Theatre, the Royal Court, Sydney Festival and the Lyceum Theatre on Broadway. Film and TV includes: *Casualty* (BBC), *Citizen Charlie* (RTE), *Sunset Song* directed by Terence Davies, *Body of Lies* directed by Ridley Scott, *Hippie Hippie Shake* directed by Beeban Kidron, *Dorothy Mills*, *Widow's Peak*, *Space Truckers*.

Sabine Dargent

has won two Irish Times Best Set Design Awards and been nominated for two others. She is a freelance set and costume designer, working mostly in theatre, with various directors and companies. Sabine has designed a few times for Jim Culleton and Fishamble Theatre Company which she always enjoys. As well as other shows for Jim, including *Monged*, *Strandline*, *Tiny Plays for Ireland 1 & 2*, and *Spinning*, she designed set and costumes for *The Pride of Parnell Street*, also written by Sebastian Barry, and designed by the same team. Sabine works with Mikel Murfi very often, also for Michael Keegan Dolan, Conall Morrison, Enda Walsh, Paul Mc Enaney, Selina Cartmell, and many others in Ireland and abroad. Some productions she has designed have been very successful and enjpoyed long tours, such as *Swan Lake*, *The Walworth Farce*, *Rian*, *The Pride of Parnell Street* . . . She loves theatre, dance, and physical theatre, but has also designed for exhibitions, films, and for big events such as the GAA 2016 celebration in Croke Park, and street theatre, such as the St Patrick's Dublin Parade sections *City Fusion* and *Brighter*, taking care of the visuals for costumes, floats, props, and make-up, for about 200 participants. Her website is www.sabinedargent.com

Mark Galione

Mark's designs in Ireland include works for Irish Modern Dance Theatre, CoisCéim, Dance Theatre of Ireland, the Peacock, Fíbín, Hands Turn, Classic Stage Ireland, Barabbas, Vesuvius, the Derry Playhouse, The Ark, Peer to Peer, Gonzo, Theatre Lovett, Second Age Theatre Company, Barnstorm, Riot and I'm Your Man for THISISPOPBABY, and for Fishamble: The New Play Company most recently *Swing* and *Inside The GPO*. Recent TV includes *Jack Lukeman 27 Club*, *All Ireland Schools Talent Search*, TG4 – *Country Music Legends* and *The All Porter Christmas Show RTE2*. Mark is a staff Lighting Designer at High Res Lighting.

Denis Clohessy

has previously worked with Fishamble, including the productions *The Pride of Parnell Street*, *Silent*, *Underneath*, *Spinning*, *Mainstream* and *Strandline*. He has also produced work for theatre and dance with the Abbey Theatre, the Gate Theatre, Rough Magic, Corn Exchange, Junk Ensemble and many others. He won the Irish Times theatre award for Best Design Sound in 2011 for Rough Magic's *Sodome, My Love*, he was a nominee in 2015 for Junk Ensemble's *It Folds*, was an associate artist with the Abbey in 2008 and a participant on Rough Magic's ADVANCE programme in 2012. His work in film and television includes the films *Older than Ireland* (Snack Box Films), *The Irish Pub* (Atom Films), *His and Hers* (Venom Film), *The Land of the Enlightened* (Savage Film), *In View* (Underground Cinema), *The Reluctant Revolutionary* (Underground Films) and the television series *Limits of Liberty* (South Wind Blows) performed by the RTE Concert Orchestra.

Stephen Bourke

is a freelance Production Manager. Stephen Studied theatre at Bull Alley, and went on to work with Bedrock for several years. He was part of the founding company of the Dublin Fringe Festival, and later was Director of Technical Services at Project Art Centre. After a period of corporate work, he made a return to the theatre and has since worked with Dear Amber (*Stones in His Pockets*), Breda Cashe (*Little Gem* tour), The Lir (*Gradfest 14, 16, 17* and others) as well as numerous other shows, events and venues. Stephen is currently Production Manager in The Complex.

Steph Ryan

has worked in theatre for many years and with many companies over the years, including Rough Magic, CoisCéim, Abbey/Peacock Theatres, OTC, to name a few. Work with Fishamble includes: *Handel's Crossing*, *The End of the Road*, *Noah and the Tower Flower*, *Spinning*, *Little Thing Big Thing*, *Invitation to a Journey* (co-production with CoisCéim, Crash Ensemble and GIAF), *Mainstream*, and Pat Kinevane's *Forgotten*, *Silent* and *Underneath*. She's delighted to be back working with Fishamble on *On Blueberry Hill*.

Tara Doolan

is a production stage manager and event manager. Recent work includes *Overshadowed* and *My Name is Saoirse* (Sunday's Child), *Sleeping Beauty* (UCH Ltd. and RCK Productions), *Charolais* (Bigger Picture Projects), *Assembly Festival*, *Underneath* and *Inside the GPO* (Fishamble: The New Play Company), *The River* (Viva Voce), *Proms in the Park*, *European Powerchair Championship Opening Ceremonies*, *No Fit State* and *Feurza Bruta*, *St Patrick's Day Parade 2014*, *Music Generation Limerick*, (Events 2013 to present), *Launch Limerick National City of Culture*, *What Happened Bridgie Cleary* (Bottom Dog Theatre Company), *Theatre at the Savoy* and *Elemental Arts and Culture Festival*. Tara is also the General Manager of Honest Arts Production Company and has acted as a stage director, writer and producer for original productions *Brian Boru: Education through Perfomance*, *The Mid-Knight Cowboy* and *Waiting in Line* which won the Cutting Edge Artist Awardat the Toronto Fringe Festival 2015.

Gavin Kostick

works as Literary Manager of Fishamble with writers for theatre through development for production, scripts, readings, mentorship programmes and a variety of courses and workshops. Gavin is also a playwright who has written over twenty plays which have been produced in Ireland and internationally. As a performer he appeared in Joseph Conrad's *Heart of Darkness: Complete*, a six-hour show in Dublin and London. In all of these areas he has gained multiple awards.

Eva Scanlan

Eva is the General Manager and Producer at Fishamble: The New Play Company. Recent, current, and upcoming work includes Fishamble's award-winning *Pat Kinevane Trilogy* on tour in Ireland and internationally, *Charolais* by Noni Stapleton at 59E59 Theaters in New York, *Maz and Bricks* by Eva O'Connor, *The Humours of Bandon* by Margaret McAuliffe, *Inside the GPO* by Colin Murphy, and *Tiny Plays for Ireland* and America at the Kennedy Centre in Washington DC and the Irish Arts Centre in New York. Eva produces T*he 24 Hour Plays: Dublin* at the Abbey Theatre in Ireland (2012–present), in association with the 24 Hour Play Company, New York, and has worked on *The 24 Hour Plays* on Broadway and *The 24 Hour Musicals* at the Gramercy Theatre. Previously, she was Producer of terraNOVA Collective in New York (2012–2015), where she produced *Underland* by Alexandra Collier (59E59 Theaters), *Social Security* by Christina Masciotti (Bushwick Starr), *terraNOVA Rx: Four Plays* in rep at IRT Theater, the soloNOVA Arts Festival, *Woman of Leisure and Panic* (FringeNYC), and *P.S. Jones and the Frozen City* (New Ohio), among other projects. Other Irish work includes *At 'the Ford* for RISE Productions, and *I'm Your Man* for Project Arts Centre and THISISPOPBABY (Dublin Theatre Festival 2015).

About Fishamble: The New Play Company

Fishamble is an Olivier Award-winning, internationally acclaimed Irish theatre company, which discovers, develops and produces new work across a range of scales. Fishamble is committed to touring throughout Ireland and internationally, and does so through partnerships and collaborations with a large network of venues, festivals and non-arts organisations.

Fishamble has earned a reputation as 'a global brand with international theatrical presence' (*Irish Times*), 'forward-thinking Fishamble' (*New York Times*), 'acclaimed Irish company' (*Scotsman*) and 'excellent Fishamble . . . Ireland's terrific Fishamble' (*Guardian*) through touring its productions to audiences in Ireland as well as to England, Scotland, Wales, France, Germany, Iceland, Croatia, Belgium, Czech Republic, Switzerland, Bulgaria, Romania, Serbia, Turkey, Finland, USA, Canada, New Zealand and Australia.

Fishamble and Pat Kinevane won an Olivier Award in 2016. Other awards for Fishamble productions include Scotsman Fringe First, Herald Angel, Argus Angel, 1st Irish, The Stage, Adelaide Fringe Best Theatre, Dublin Fringe, Forbes' Best Theater, Stage Raw LA, and Irish Times Theatre Awards, as well as Irish Writer's Guild/ZeBBie and Stewart Parker Trust awards for many of its playwrights. Fishamble's living archive is in the National Library of Ireland.

Fishamble is at the heart of new writing for theatre in Ireland, not just through its productions, but through its extensive programme of training, development and mentoring schemes. These include the *New Play Clinic*, and Irish Times Theatre Award 2017 nominated *Show in a Bag* which is run in partnership with Dublin Fringe Festival and Irish Theatre Institute. Each year, Fishamble typically supports 60 per cent of the writers of all new plays produced on the island of Ireland, approximately 55 plays each year.

Fishamble is funded by the Arts Council and Dublin City Council.
Its international touring is supported by Culture Ireland.

Fishamble's recent and current productions include:

On Blueberry Hill by Sebastian Barry (2017)

Maz and Bricks by Eva O'Connor (2017)

The Humours of Bandon by Margaret McAuliffe (2017)
on national and international tour

Charolais by Noni Stapleton (2017) in New York

Inside the GPO by Colin Murphy (2016)
performed in the GPO at Easter

Tiny Plays for Ireland and America by 26 writers (2016)
at the Kennedy Center, Washington DC, and Irish Arts Center,
New York, as part of *Ireland 100*

Mainstream by Rosaleen McDonagh (2016)
in co-production with Project Arts Centre

Invitation to a Journey by David Bolger,
Deirdre Gribbin and Gavin Kostick (2016)
in co-production with CoisCeim, Crash Ensemble
and Galway International Arts Festival

Underneath by Pat Kinevane (since 2014)
touring in Ireland, UK, Europe, US, Australia

Little Thing, Big Thing by Donal O'Kelly (2014–16)
touring in Ireland, UK, Europe, New York, Australia

Silent by Pat Kinevane (since 2011)
touring in Ireland, UK, Europe, US, Australia

Swing by Steve Blount, Peter Daly, Gavin Kostick
and Janet Moran (2014–16) touring in Ireland,
UK, Europe, US, Australia and New Zealand

Forgotten by Pat Kinevane (since 2007)
touring in Ireland, UK, Europe, US

Spinning by Deirdre Kinahan (2014)
at Dublin Theatre Festival

The Wheelchair on My Face by Sonya Kelly,
(2013–14) touring in Ireland, UK, Europe, US

Fishamble Staff

Artistic Director   Jim Culleton
General Manager   Eva Scanlan
Literary Manager   Gavin Kostick
Marketing and Fundraising Executive   Chandrika Narayanan-Mohan

Fishamble Board

Tania Banotti, Padraig Burns, Elizabeth Davis, Peter Finnegan,
Doireann Ní Bhriain, Vincent O'Doherty, John O'Donnell,
Siobhan O'Leary, Andrew Parkes (Chair).

Fishamble wishes to thank the following
Friends of Fishamble for their invaluable support

Alan & Rosemarie Ashe, Halsey and Sandra Beemer, Mary Banotti,
Tania Banotti, Colette Bowles Breen, Padraig Burns, Maura Connolly,
Ray Dolphin, John Fanagan, Barbara FitzGerald, Cora Fitzsimons,
Pauline Gibney, Ann Glynn, Eithne Healy, John and Yvonne Healy,
The Georganne Aldrich Heller Foundation, Gillie Hinds,
Jane and Geoffrey Keating, Lisney, Richard McCullough,
Aidan Murphy, Liz Nugent, Lucy Nugent, Patrick Molloy,
Dympna Murray, Vincent O'Doherty, Joanna Parkes, Nancy Pasley,
Georgina Pollock, David and Veronica Rowe, Colleen Savage,
Mary Sheerin, Grace Smith, Claudia Carroll.

Thank you also to all those who do not wish to be credited.

www.fishamble.com
www.facebook.com/fishamble
www.twitter.com/fishamble

Acknowledgements

Thanks to the following for their help with this production:
Rachel West and all at the Arts Council;
Hugh Murray and everyone at Pavilion;
Willie White and everyone at Dublin Theatre Festival;
Sinéad Mac Aodha, Nora Hickey M'Sichili and
everyone at Centre Culturel Irlandais; Maureen Kennelly
and all at Poetry Irelandand; and all those who have helped
since this publication went to print.

On Blueberry Hill

Sebastian Barry was born in 1955 and educated at Catholic University School and Trinity College, Dublin. For his plays he has won a number of awards, including a Critics' Circle Award and Lloyd's Private Banking Playwright of the Year. For his novels he has been awarded the Costa Book of the Year Award (twice), the Walter Scott Prize (twice), the James Tait Black Memorial Prize, and has been twice shortlisted for the Booker Prize. He has honorary doctorates from the Open University, NUI Galway, and the University of East Anglia.

SEBASTIAN BARRY

On Blueberry Hill

FABER & FABER

First published in 2017
by Faber and Faber Ltd
74–77 Great Russell Street
London WC1B 3DA

Typeset by Country Setting, Kingsdown, Kent CT14 8ES
Printed in England by CPI Group (UK) Ltd, Croydon CRO 4YY

A CIP record for this book is available from the British Library

978-0-571-34292-1

FSC
www.fsc.org
MIX
Paper from
responsible sources
FSC® C013604

2 4 6 8 10 9 7 5 3 1

On Blueberry Hill was first produced by Fishamble at the Pavilion Theatre, Dún Laoghaire, as part of the Dublin Theatre Festival, on 27 September 2017. The cast was as follows:

Christy Niall Buggy
PJ David Ganly

Directed by Jim Culleton
Set and Costume Design by Sabine Dargent
Lighting Design by Mark Galione
Sound Design by Denis Clohessy
Produced by Eva Scanlan

Characters

PJ
Christy

ON BLUEBERRY HILL

*This play went to press while the production
was still in rehearsal, so will not reflect
any late changes to the script*

*A prison cell, narrow and old. There's a bunk bed. It's
pretty bare otherwise. There's a radio, with yellowed
Sellotape keeping it together. There's an old black Bible
on one of the bunk beds. The wall above the other has a
few cut-outs of page-three girls. Ronan Collins is talking
on the radio about Fats Domino's birthday.*

*The occupants of the cell are a grey-haired man, in his
late fifties, somewhat fat, Dublin middle-class accent,
PJ, and a slighter man, maybe ten years older, Christy,
working-class accent, balding.*

*Direct address to us, but also, somewhat aware of each
other.*

PJ

Ann so tosach do bhí an briathar.

There I am – I can almost see myself – a young fella at
Maynooth, walking along the cinder path, under the host
of beech trees. With my Gaelic Bible, the wind snatching
at the flimsy paper. The paper like the stuff they used to
wrap a loaf in, in a country shop. The yellowness of it.
There was something in the paper that meant it was
always yellow but I couldn't tell you what. There must
have been a factory somewhere, God knows where, in the
midlands maybe, making that paper.

Walking there, the picture of goodness.

Then, much much earlier, in the sixties, I remember
coming in from school and my mother was crying in the
kitchen with the newspaper and I asked her what was the

matter, and she said Kennedy had been killed, and I burst into tears. But I had no idea who Kennedy was, he could have been the local grocer. It was her own tears that slayed me.

I suppose the murderous bits of the sixties never really reached us, we were too far away from everything. Nevertheless, the sixties – like the whole world stuck its finger in an electric plug. In those days you could do a thing like that. You could stick your finger straight in. Parents lived in fear of things like that. But not too much else. Safety. In my childhood we still roamed about, we still climbed trees. We more or less nested in them. You could climb to the top of a great oak and build a house in it and no one would say boo to you. That sort of thing was encouraged.

There was no safety in plugs and the like of that, but there was another sort of safety.

You never heard of a child falling out of a tree. You never saw anything like that.

Everyone went to Mass, everyone believed in God.

My mother was put to the pin of her collar when Daddy died, we had only his civil service pension then, we had no extra funds, we had no motor car, but what was that to us, we never went too far.

And when we did, on holidays in Mayo as may be, she always had the lend of a pony and trap from her Uncle Thaddy.

With the great lamp out in front, in the darkness, lighting our way along the metalled roads.

And the green roads still, here and there. I remember my mother, well I do remember it, in her thin summer dress, battling along on the trap, the reins lofted high, with the pony a wretch, a wretch at every turn. My mother's bare arms as blonde as hurleys. Her shouting at Billie the pony, 'Pull up, pull up, the boy!' But yahooing herself, you know, on the leafy, dark back-roads, where no one could hear her, excepting myself, aged nine – two stumpy legs like ninepins, me hollering also inside the storm of her own shouting.

And to 'Maison Prost' for the 'French schoolboy' haircut. She would run her hand through the surviving eighth of an inch of hair. Embarrassing me, greatly. 'Oh, just like a French schoolboy.' Now, Mr Prost's family had been in Ireland for a hundred years. He'd probably never set foot in his native country. And she had certainly never been to France to be observing the haircuts of schoolboys. But the name alone inspired her.

Maison Prost.

That sort of thing gave her joy.

Half the pleasure of life is not thinking about it too much.

In those days, the old certainties remained. We hated the English. I mean, at my secondary school, soccer was banned. Association football. Because, they 'associated' it with England, the priests did. We played soccer in the yard of course – like maniacs. But for proper matches, it was all rugby.

Rugby, that well-known game of Celtic origin.

We hated the English but that didn't mean we loved ourselves.

We spoke English, but we were learning the Irish – eventually, you know, to get it back. Government jobs, you had to have the Irish. Postmen, you know. Teachers. People like that. Actors. Prison guards.

Focail is the Irish for 'word'. We used to love saying that in class. *Briathar* is another word for 'word', but there's no fun to be had in that.

Ann so tosach do bhí an briathar.

Christy

We were crowded at the window, seven faces, my sisters and brothers and the ma herself, looking out, at Da, fighting at the gate with that daft cousin of his, Con Daly, and the two of them wrestling for a long while, in the summer mud of the road, then the bodies banging about against the concrete wall of the garden, very awkward-looking and painful to my seven-year-old eyes, and the neighbours looking out their windows the other side of the road, and I saw a man standing in one of the gardens, then *withdrawing* himself into the house, as if he was afraid somehow, and then, at the end of all, with a last great effort, my da heaving his arm up as if it was a great weight by then, to stop the blow of Daly's knife coming down on his chest, but he miscalculated, or hadn't the energy to deflect it, and it went in, deep, into Da's breast, it might have touched his heart, we in the window gasped out, and Ma screamed, put her hands over her face, Jesus, I remember that for some reason, and then the guards came running down the road, I suppose they had come hot-foot up from Monkstown. It was a feud fight, my father was *beholden* to answer the challenge from Con Daly, he had no choice in a matter like that, my da was a tinker, the most famous tinker in that time, because he was as big as a dray, and Con Daly his match, and they fought it out, like it was a cowboy at the Adelphi, for fuck's sake, and the upshot of it was, my da was killed. He was twenty-six.

I'd far sooner forget that, except, in another way, I hold on to it because it's the last time I saw my da.

So then it was just the ma grappling for the bit of money to feed and clothe us and that wasn't easy, it must have been queer hard for her betimes, I would say, and as each of us reached fourteen, we would just leave the school and go get whatever jobs we could, anything. Me, I got a job caddying up at the posh golf course which was actually not too far from where we lived, just the top of the road there as it heads for the wilds of Dalkey. It was a grand little job really, and the tips were often surprising – I mean, shocking even. I came home once with a ten-shilling note, one of those red jobs, an English one, because in them days you could use both, it was given me by this old chap was in the films that time, it was like nineteen sixty or something, so I was fifteen roundabout, he shot this wonderful round of golf, so he did, in the wide blaze of a summer's day, I don't think I ever saw a man so happy till that moment, really happy he was, gazing at the score card, gazing at the big heap of sun lying all over Dunleary below, and him laughing, with his little leprechaun laugh, and hadn't he played a leprechaun or something, in *Darby McGill* was it, or the friend of a fucking leprechaun, ah, yes, he was a lovely man, Barry Fitzgerald was his name, he's probably forgotten now. But I remember him. When the ma saw the ten-bob note she went white in the face, she thought I had nicked it out of the dairy, because they still kept cows there, and had a fucking meadow, and it was well known that they kept the money in an ould decorative churn, because your man Dempsey what owned it didn't trust banks, but I hadn't, no, it was your man the leprechaun gave it to me, though I'd have robbed the Hibernian Bank for her, if she'd have needed me to, I'd have robbed Fort Knox.

So inspired by this success in my career, I took the old mailboat to England. Everyone got so drunk on that journey the floor of the boat was a sea of black porter, puked up by the drinkers, and I don't know how, but still black, you know, and down in the hold of the ship were these huge state rooms, with low roofs, and what looked to my young eyes like a hundred bunks in each, three tiers of them like in a fucking concentration camp, and all these ould builders in them, sleeping, dozing, drunk as monks, with the boots on the floor and the big socks still on their feet, stuck like, showing the holes, because a lot of these lads had no women to be darning holes, and anyhow, you'd have needed a long cleft stick to touch those items, such was the almighty dirt of them, hundreds of mouldy thick grey socks, builders' socks you might say, and when you stepped in the cabin, by Jesus, the stink, the almighty stink would fell a bullock. And that's how they looked on us, you know, really, the poor English, the shock we gave them, the mailboat was called the cattle boat as everyone knows, and we were the cattle. I don't remember one girl in all that cargo, but there must have been girls, going working in England, heifers I suppose we must say, hidden away in the ship somewhere. I just remember the big men.

But when you went working on the buildings you discovered that these men, many of them, were geniuses, they could do very skilled work, amazing really, proper plastering now, that's very tricky, you should try it sometime, you'll soon find out the hardship of it, and real brickwork, laying beautiful courses, decorative work oftentimes in London, oh, yes, geniuses, and I watched them closely and learned everything I eventually knew off of them, which was very handy. And the big thing on a building site is, if they ask you can you do something, you always say yes, or I always did, and one time it was 'Can you drive a dozer?' and I said yes, sure I had the bit of practice on a pal's motorcycle in Ireland, and then another time, when I had mastered the dozer, and I did fucking master it, it was, 'Can you drive a crane?' and of course I said yes, and climbed up this skinny metal ladder, up a hundred feet, with my legs trembling, into this little cabin, swaying in the wind, and Jesus, I soon worked out the handles and gears, through my tears, fucking scared to death I was, but sure it's just common sense, trial and error, if you use the noggin you can do it. Driving a crane is good money because it's so fucking dangerous, talk about fucking skilled work, for fuck's sake.

PJ

We went out, Peadar and myself, to the island. A day as rare as hens' teeth, with armies of sunlight and shadows advancing and retreating everywhere.

I had met him on an annual retreat, he was just a local boy, from the other side of Monkstown, thought he had a vocation. I spotted him on the first day, he was talking to the attendant priests, sort of one by one, I thought, as if looking for something, a sign maybe, or an indication. A perfectly normal young Irish boy except he was shining with beauty. To me, anyway. I have no idea what he looked like to other people. I couldn't even have said those words to myself, then, 'shining with beauty'. Nor anything close to them. But it was so.

God knows.

With an accent on him that would mash spuds. Monkstown Farm he was from, council houses. You wouldn't go up there without a native guide, you could be murdered crossing Dunedin Field on your own, if they didn't know you.

I call him a boy, though he was seventeen years of age, just a few years younger than myself. I could account myself a man, a young man, but there was little of the man about Peadar, in appearance. He was so slim, slight, a little girlish really, a sort of waif, but full of a signalling

17

power. Maybe timeless is the word I want, there was nothing of the child in him, nothing of the man, like a marble statue, glowing, vibrant, but also frozen – eternal. Yes, eternal, was what I meant to say.

Love, you see, love – well, no one has ever found proper words for that, not really. It's the thing God wants us to have, to embody, and yet there is no proper description of it.

The first time I saw him, I thought, 'Uh-ho, there's trouble.' I didn't know why I thought that. Well, I didn't know anything. I was just after finishing my third year at the seminary. I *thought* I knew everything. If I could properly describe him I think everything would be understood. But God didn't give us words for it.

We went out to the island. The big island on Aran, Inishmore. Well, we had to find somewhere to be together, I mean, without comment, visitors, two young men going out on the ferry, walkers as might be, seminarians, religious, devout. I mean, Ireland was full of them then, there were hundreds and hundreds of young priests and priesteens, must have been thousands. Everywhere in Ireland, cycling, walking, there were young gossoons, dressed soberly, blackly. And we went out to the island in that guise, like two ordinary lads, to sample the simple pleasure of being in an ancient landscape, with the lovely music of Irish around us in the mouths of the people.

I am telling the story, and then, my mind goes like a darting bird to what happened, not quite next, but a little later, flies ahead, and –

In that time my mother was about forty-five years old. Yes, Daddy had died long since, he had been weakened by polio as a child. He was a great race-goer while he lived. He always brought me back a pear from the pram-women who would be selling pears at the meetings, but in the matter of his life he was a poor bet, I suppose he was, and he succumbed, I was told, but to what I didn't register, or forget. A child has different ears to an adult. But he left her a little house in Monkstown, and she worked in Ballsbridge for the Sweepstakes. She put on a bit of weight and she didn't care, she said, because she wasn't planning to marry again, despite her being a bit of a looker, in all honesty, which was one of the things I liked about her when I was boy. When I was little she still looked like she was in her twenties, they thought she was my sister at the school gates. And not very religious, as you might expect of a seminarian's mother, but she liked old churches, she longed to go to Italy someday to see what she called 'real churches', with proper paintings in them, not like the Irish ones with the job-lots of St Josephs and stiff madonnas. So she said. She had a nice high way of talking, I don't think there was any harm in her.

She had these old seventy-eights she played on the huge gramophone Daddy had bought, Hoagy Carmichael 'Down in Old Hong Kong', 'The Old Music Master' who just sat there amazed. (*Singing.*) 'Wide-eyed and open mouthed he gazed and he gazed.' But at what I don't remember. Daddy's old records were things like Mussorgsky, 'Pictures at an Exhibition', a whole set of ten records like ten black plates, in brown paper sleeves all worn and torn, but she never touched them after he died. In the summer I remember she brought me on the train, we would catch it at Monkstown station, out to Dalkey, and we went down the hundred steps to the beach at White Rock, herself and myself, and she laid herself out on an accommodating rock to get the sun, and I walked the whole beach leaping from boulder to boulder, adroitly, or so I imagined. And she had brought fourpenny bars of Cadbury's chocolate which would be melted in their wrappers in a very agreeable way. And then when I was older she let me climb over the big cliff at the end of the beach and penetrate on to Killiney Strand, into a new kingdom of experience, and I would go happily, as happy as I ever was at any time in my life, to the little shop where the hanging chalets were, and the long concrete slipway like a woman's throat, and the handsome fellas hiring out rowing boats, and buy the bottle of Savage Smith orange as cold as your nose in winter. And I would traipse back with that, and drink it on the pebbly sand beside her, raging, raging with happiness.

I remember things like that. Whether they cause me pain or happiness now I couldn't say. It seems a long long time ago.

Now here we are, Christy and me. An odd life, no doubt. How could it be otherwise?

(*Looking around.*) Doesn't look much, I know. Used to be a table in here, but Christy tore a leg off it, trying to fix the blasted thing.

Christy

Ancient fucking history. Coming home from England, the bit of money in the pocket, meeting the wife. Well, I suppose I could tell you how that happened. It was in the Monument Creamery, in Dunleary, she had a job there, not out on the floor of course, with her accent, you know, bringing teas and cakes to the good citizens, but yeah, the usual, slopping out, and all the rest of it. There's a lot of rough stuff goes on in the background of every business, even a nice café. And one morning she comes out into the lane at the back of premises, with her big bucket, and there was what she described after as 'a long, thin rasher of a man' lying there, sleeping, and I was in her way across to the bins, real smelly they were too, and so she gives me a kick, just to get me moving. 'Would you get up, get up, whoever you are, you can't be lying there like a cat.' So I goes up on one elbow and look at her. No messing now, she was a fabulous-looking girl. She was so pretty she was walking in her own bleeding light, that's how it was, with blondy hair and lovely dark skin like a fucking Galway woman, though her people were all from Old Dunleary, they worked in the coalyard there, three generations, several. That evening I came back for her, I cleaned myself up a bit, I'd been on a terrible razzle right enough, drinking around the town for three weeks, money in my pocket, you know. And I walked her home along the seafront, past the railway wall and the coal quay inside Monkstown harbour, and in she goes and comes out in due course all washed and kitted out in that lovely summer dress, and she was only a small woman, seventeen, by Christ we went dancing in the Top Hat, we danced all evening, and I bought her lemonade, which was all the fuckers would sell you at the bar, Fats Domino was all the rage then, she danced so well, much better than me, though I had a go, just for the look of it, 'I found my freedom, on Blueberry Hill, on Blueberry Hill, when I found you'. Oh my God, the romance. I was crazy about her. And it didn't take much more than that. She felt the same and we tied the knot, and my ma was still alive in that time and she brought the smaller childer, she made dresses and suits for them, yes she did, and Christine, which funnily enough was my wife's name, considering my name is Christy, she still had that light of hers, going through the ceremony, Father fucking Murphy that later done time for his sins, and she beaming, like the little lighthouse at the end of the pier, and having the feed at the Pierre Hotel, and us all coming out into the late twilight of a summer's night, happy as larks with the skinful of beer and burnt chicken, oh yes, and the wide bay lying there before us like the bedclothes of God. And then, one thing following another, in immemorial fashion as you might say, the kids came, Mickey, Doreen and Peadar. Cock of the walk, me then, having my pints in Carneys in the evenings, plenty of money and mates, enjoying the work on the buildings. Be nice to have that back. Yesh, when I think of all that, I think, be nice to have all that back. Be fucking nice. Ordinary life, you could call it. Being young. And your kids young. It's a special time when you're young and your kids are small. But you don't really know it. You're in the dead centre of things. Like a dart on the dartboard. The bull's-eye. You've hit the fucking bull's-eye of life and you don't really know it. That's the beauty of it maybe. You're young, you can drink twenty pints in a night and barely feel it in the morning, go off to work at six in the dawn light, with your fucking sandwiches and your billycan of tea, fucking brilliant, and in through the site gate with a wave from the gateman, and booking in with the gaffer, and off you go with the day's slog, mixing the muck, fixing lines for the block work, digging out trenches for pipework till you're fair weeping from exhaustion, the pain in your back, the wrench in your legs, and swapping jokes till your gums bleed, but at the centre of everything, fuck it, you're happy, your wife is as pretty as a film star, a little beauty from Old Dunleary, and your daughter, oh by Jesus, what a shock to you she is, something you made, not with your bare hands, but something you made, and the fucking pride in your little sons, thinking about them, what they would be doing in the world, maybe going out building like yourself, ah, Jesus, I don't know, sometimes life is stacked up all right, all your ducks in a row, and in the summer the sun is shining, and in the winter frost gnaws at your gloves, why is all that so fucking marvellous, but it is, better than steak every day, better than any fucking thing you can think of, ordinary fucking life, and when I am talking about it now, I am yearning for it, I am yearning for it.

PJ

But, we went out to the island, Peadar and I. I have either two memories of it, or else as it happened two separate things happened simultaneously, which I know is not possible. I know what I said at the time, and I know why I said it, but that's not really the point now. If I could go back to the second before it happened, and choose another outcome, or even be sure of what exactly took place, I would, gladly.

So I will try to say what took place, and perhaps by the very saying, see it again, and know for sure what happened.

We took the little ferry, marvelling at the beauty of the sea between Rossaveal and Kilronan, the way the sea itself seemed to dive down beneath itself, resurfacing, resurfacing, as if the entire body of the water were a stupendous grey whale – took ourselves off at the little jetty, walked across the strand below the tattered village, heading for the other side of the bay, where our map showed a rough path that would take us to the cliffs at the back of the island. There might be remnants of antiquities there, not the famous Dun Aengus, but some lesser spot. Rarely seen and rarely visited, our guidebook said, which spurred Peadar's curiosity. I was delighted to follow him.

I say this and immediately wonder if it was so. Was I not also vaguely angry with him, wanting to take the more usual road to the tremendous cliffs at Dun Aengus, maybe hire a pony and trap, relishing the clop-clop of the hooves on the stony road? Was I not even a little impatient with him, his lengthening stride along the sand, his blissful youthfulness, a quality which though I was patently young myself I had never really possessed. Was there not also a deeper anger, born out of a hatred of myself, what I was, what he was? Could it even be said I despised him,

though I was half of the equation now that made him up
– myself almost ludicrous in my own eyes, a tubby man
in clerical garb traipsing after a willowy figure in his own
dark clothes, me sweating in my solemn coat, my body
not trim and hard like his, but soft, flabby, slow. Or was
I as I say delighted, maybe even transfigured by the day,
the beautiful, chaotic, tumbling mix of wind and sunlight
blowing us along our way, clouds intervening briefly, then
light again, the sand darkening and lightening, the sea
also, and also the side-view of his face, clean-shaven, his
skin permanently darkened by previous sunlight, as if he
had harvested the meagre rations of it all summer long,
and stored it in his skin? Did I not grievously love him, or
did I resent that love, as being sinful, indeed prohibited
by the state, liable to all sorts of punishments, public
opprobrium, deepest shame, prison sentences? Was the
union of the wind and sun really able in those moments
to calm my self-tormenting brain, and release me into
simple love, simple desire? We had been going about for
six months, creatures in love, of course we were, except,
where was that love ultimately to exist, where was the
damn chapel, the priest, to wed us, what were the words
that would be said, what was the strange congregation
that would come to celebrate us, well no one and
nowhere, nothing, not ever, not for us . . .

Was that what I was thinking, or all those things at once,
as if our thoughts were another version of that sea, far
out, diving deviously beneath itself, like Moby Dick
himself?

We got to the cliffs. The land was lower there, there was
a modesty to the place. Because we were unobserved, we
lay down in a hollow for a little while. Then it was back
to the antiquities. Peadar was excited, because he could
make out old stones on the ground, like a strange road,
but more likely the foundations of a Celtic fort. And he

said he was pleased that no archaeologists had come out
to rebuild it, in the years since independence, as they had
in other places. The old stones ended at the cliff, a drop
of fifty feet to the water below. We watched a gannet
fishing in the swell, disappearing as it went down for fish,
reappearing then suddenly many yards from its original
spot. Peadar was standing there, excited, passionate, on
the edge of the cliff. I remember worrying about the
ground beneath his feet, it might have been just a thin
shelf of rock, how could we tell? A devious wind came up
behind us, he was caught off guard, off balance, and he
tottered forward an inch or two. And I reached out to
steady him. That was my first intention. But suddenly
something else gripped me. Assailed me. A queer little
instinct to push him off. Help him on his way with a little
push. Why in God's name did I want to do that? I don't
know, I don't know. When I look into my heart, I can see
no answer, only a black little mark against my soul. Not
an instinct much to do with anything, a strange little
instinct like something from childhood, a sudden
capricious wickedness, a piece of wretched divilment.
And on this tiny moment turned my whole life.

Over he went, inexorable as you like, Peadar, his face in
profile to me, turning from gladness to horror, he uttered
something, he said something to me, 'PJ, PJ, catch me,
catch me!' and I am sure I tried to catch him then, I am
sure I did. But the laws of gravity were against us, and
you know, no one falls slowly, you are gone in a moment,
a fraction of a moment. I don't even know if I touched
his jacket again, he was gone, over the edge, down down
to the sea, Peadar, falling, falling, and me peering over
after him, he fell like a wounded bird, plummeting,
screaming, and bounced twice on rocks protruding, and
struck the Atlantic with hardly a sound, far away below,
and was gobbled, gobbled you would think, by the
strange greed of the sea. And I was screaming myself.

And just then, though I hadn't spotted them, hadn't noticed them at all even in that bare expanse of peat and rock, two older priests suddenly appeared at my side, and maybe, truth to tell, prevented me from throwing myself after him, for that is exactly what I wanted to do. 'Oh, my God, your friend has fallen in,' the first man said. 'I pushed him, I pushed him,' I cried, crying out like a confessing criminal broken on the rack of a long interrogation, but no, hadn't he only just uttered his few words, and the other priest, a small bony chap, stepped back from me in that instant, as if, having killed one man, I might be of a mind to kill two.

Christy

What was I supposed to do? Is there no honour in the world? There is. My own father, that fought to the death with Con Daly, fought for his honour. It was all about honour, the tinker's life, I tell you. And I was the son of a tinker man, and by Jesus going back to the time of Jesus Christ, tinkers all, father to father. We made the nails that went into His hands and feet, to hold the poor man up on the cross, and that's why we were put to wandering, it was a punishment right enough, but it was honour too, to meet your fate like a man, OK, we done wrong, but here's what we are now, fucking fine tinkerfolk of the finest sort, can do any job for you, any feat of strength, 'Can you drive a crane?' 'I can.' Go anywhere and live off the countryside, you know, in the old days, mend a bucket here, a basin there, and the women walking about, asking for butter and eggs at the farmhouse doors, this-and-that from the *bean-an-tí*. It is two thousand years since we made them nails, and holy bloody people we were always, my father's people. Honour, honour, my boys.

Was I to let it go by, as if it never happened?

I know it's a terrible thing, well I know it.

And don't think for a moment it was easily done, but fury brought me through it, the fury of a father.

But not just at the start. At the start it was all very different. Because you know, you're in shock. But there's nothing like a trial in the Four Courts to cure you of shock. I was just listening to lies. Lies from dawn to dusk. You never heard such a palaver from a lawyer. Now, fair dues, he pleaded guilty, and he was definitely going down, but by God, we had to hear the four fucking gospels of St PJ first, God forgive me. What a great fucking chap he was, so out of character, blah blah blah. And ould priests coming up from Maynooth, crispy-looking lads dragged up in midlands shops no doubt, sliced pan and duck's eggs, you know the sort, blathering about PJ, and the great vocation he had, like there were classes of fucking vocation, and his was at the top of the pile. Holy Jesus Christ he was going to be, apparently, probably Archbishop of Armagh at close of play, if not Bishop of fucking Rome, but for this small little matter of having killed my son.

Killed my son. Did they not understand that? That Peadar's father was sitting in that room, listening to their gobbledygook lies? About his this and his that – his *nature* as the lawyer said, this fucking beer-keg of a creature in an oily black cloak, roly-poly fucking high-falutin talking on him, like he knew him or something, like he would ever have known him in a month of Sundays, how he had risen above his – what was the word he used? Ah, yes, his origin. His origin, and him the grandson of tinker royalty. How the fuck would he know, how the fuck would he know? Yes, I was quite calm and reasonable going in, Christine said as much, because she worried I would go fucking spare, but the blather out of them, the fucking talk of them, I mean, it would have tried the patience of Job.

Peadar. I don't know. Was there ever such a fine boy? He was a fine boy, so he was, even if he was going for the priesthood. I told him, I told him, Peadar, don't go near that shower of knackers, just knackers they are, sell your feet for glue, come on to the buildings with me. Now maybe I'm as fond as the next man of a decent sermon, I like to feel that terror creeping o'er me, as the song says, but that's not the point, that's not the point. Christine told him too, she said, Peadar, don't be moving away from your own people, no good can come of that, stick with your own. But Peadar, you see, was clever, I mean, he didn't know a damn thing about anything, but he was book clever. He wrote a scholarship essay for the secondary school, and he was the first boy in the history of our lot to finish the long, great slog of school, so he was. I mean, he wasn't like other boys in Monkstown Farm. He didn't want to go see Finn Harps playing Bray Wanderers at the football, he didn't give a fuck about Finn Harps and Bray Wanderers. He wanted to go into town with me to see the fucking dried-out elephants and very dead snakes in the museum in Merrion Square, with fucking half-puked-up globules of things, and stingrays and sharks poised to strike, but never to strike again, and what, the babies of marmosets in formaldehyde jars. I don't know. And then it was the train to Connolly Station, the station of the bleeding Scotsman that died for Ireland, God help us, and then cross over Gardiner Street by Talbot Street, that wore the chains next-nigh anent his skin, into Marlborough Street, and up past the Pro Cathedral, where they laid out the murdered body of Michael Collins, to where, do you think? What hallowed spot of history and legend? Well? The shop where they sold clothes to the priests. You probably often wondered where they bought those horrible black trousers, and the skimpy sweaters with the arms missing, well, I know where they bought them, because there's a shop up there on Marlborough Street, believe it or not Mr Ripley, where they sell such ravishing items of fashion. And if you want a nice black scarf, you can get one there too.

So not like other boys. But like what then? His 'nature' as the fella called it. He was soft as a hot cross bun, you know, when you buy it early on Good Friday, and it's still warm from the baker's oven, the Monument Creameries indeed, and you break it open, and you'd want a gob of butter on it too, because it is soft, soft and wonderful, just like Peadar. He knew every girl in Monkstown Farm, and every girl liked him, he wasn't trying to climb into their knickers, it was a break for them, it was a relief from the usual wrestling that went on. And he was happy to go to dances in the hall at Dunedin, of course, he was a better dancer than his mother, which is saying something, they all danced with him, they all liked him, I suppose, in all truth, he was one of them, in that he understood them better than anyone. I remember him saying once to his ma, I heard him say it, he didn't know I could hear, I was settled there in the dark of the scullery, smoking a fag, and I heard him talking to Christine about how he thought women had the worst of it, and the admiration he had for her, can you imagine that? Listening to your son saying such wise fucking things, I was gobsmacked, the fag burned down to my fingers before I noticed. Because yeah, they do, woman have it rough, I know that, yesh, pushing out babies and all the trouble with their insides, and having to bring up kids regardless, and if there isn't enough to go round, as may be, as happens now and then in all families, she'll go without, and then you have fellas coming home with a skinful of beer, and beating the living Jesus out of them, and then at the shops the next day, trying to hide the bruises with a headscarf, they'll dig out a headscarf of their mother's or their granny's, because no young one has worn a head scarf in Ireland for twenty years. So you can tell by this sudden going backwards of fashion that something is amiss. And then the fucking social worker making everything worse, I suppose, and every fucking month, every fucking month, in the grip of their period, God help the poor creatures, oh Jesus, Christine, you don't want to be in hand's distance of her when she's going through that, she's like a rattlesnake. And Peadar seemed to know all that, even though he was only a boy, wanting to be a priest. A priest, you know, and if ever a man was an ignoramus when it comes to women, it's a priest, generally, if you ask me, not that she'd say that, but how-and-ever, in my opinion. He was going to be the best priest that ever Ireland saw. In fact in my opinion my son was a sort of saint.

PJ

There was a strange between-time, before they arrested me. I ran down to Kilronan to ask for help, and the lifeboat was called on the telephone and I was told it was putting out from Rossaveal immediately, and in the meantime, two men took me round in a curach, when I say took me round, you wouldn't believe the size of the sea at the boot of the island, the waves were strange and solemn, thirty feet high, but wide and smooth, and the currach rode over them lightly, the two men with arms as thick as the legs of bulls, working the oars, bladeless oars I remember, that needed no feathering in the wind. But the sea behind the island under the cliff was glassy and basalt black, as if stricken by some ailment, and as we rowed along the rocks you could hear a seal barking, *madra na mara*, the dog of the sea, or is that the otter, I can't remember, and the gulls went round in mad swoops, diving, shrieking, protesting, to try and put you off your journey, their loved chicks hidden in high niches, and those stout birds with the yellow beaks, and the fishermen were asking me what had happened, and I was trying with all my will to tell them, and be honest about it, but I was having difficulty, maybe my head was breaking asunder, I couldn't remember and I could remember, I saw two things at once, it was like a true hallucination, and the men were so solicitous and kind in their questions, I was the friend bereaved, an imposter, and the lifeboat came near and shouted at the men to lay off, which they did, and up on the cliff top, risking their own lives, the two priests were pointing and shouting, and I saw from about a hundred yards distant three of the lifeboatmen in their yellow gabardines reach down into the water for something, and pull what looked like a sliver of the dark black sea itself up on to the deck. And that was my Peadar.

And the two priests were strangely solicitous also, I was surrounded by kindness, it was so strange, but they couldn't *unhear* what I had told them. The young guard came on to the quay, they had laid Peadar in the fish store where it was icy cold, and questioned me. God knows what I told him, and then he questioned the two priests, and they told him what I had said, as they were obliged to do. So suddenly a different complexion was put on things, and I went from bereaved friend to possible killer, and I said to the guard I had killed him, I believed I had, and when his sergeant came out on the ferry, they arrested me, and I went back with them and Peadar to the mainland, on the same ferry we had taken only hours before, in our innocent joyfulness, the evening wind striking like spears across the holds, whipping alike at the living and the dead.

Christy

The fecking guards came to the door. That's never a good feeling. I thought I was in trouble for something else entirely, and the blood drained from my arms. It's not a pretty sight, two Dunleary guards coming up your

asphalt path. Was I nearly forty then? But if I was, I hadn't
learned much sense. But sense is second in my book to
doing the right thing. Even when the right thing is the
wrong thing, if you follow me. Anyhows, there was this
rich fella I was working for by then, I used to work on
some of his building projects, just digging and fetching as
usual, but then I suppose he saw I was, I don't know,
handy with many things, and maybe he just liked me, I
don't know. He was a decent ould cuss anyhow. He was a
single man, and he lived out in a big house in Portmarnock,
with a long straight avenue and everything, Georgian
gaff, stuffed with paintings and antiques, but he had this
German bird used to come over to see him regular, and
he would send me out in his Bentley sports car to the
airport to fetch her. That was a lovely car to be driving
in, and I relished those journeys. Me, Christy, sailing
along in a yoke must have cost the best part of a hundred
grand, usually working for him I drove a Transit van.
She herself, Helga was her name, was one of those big
Germans, taller than me anyway, a big skinny queen of a
woman, nice as you like, sweet-natured. I don't know, she
was sort of what do you call it, vulnerable as the docs
say, she was nervous always, hated going through
customs, she'd be trembling when I'd meet her at the
doors, always had a bit of pot in her handbag, just to
calm herself, maybe that's what made her so jumpy. So
we would stop at that hotel in Drumcondra just beside
the walls of the institute, and take a room for the
afternoon, and ride each other like the world was ending,
lovely it was, though of course I was horrible guilty
about it, what with Christine at home with the kids. But
it was the Bentley sports car and the bloody great height
of her, I couldn't help myself. It was like I was a different
person entirely, and because she didn't speak English, she
didn't get the rough Dunleary accent off myself, she had
no idea where I was from, she just took me as she found

me, which is one of the best things about foreign travel. Foreign travel in Drumcondra.

And that was all alright, never caused any bother to no one, and it went on for a few years, and otherwise I was doing errands for your man, sorting things for him when they needed sorting, getting rid of lads on building sites that would be idling, which is a very annoying thing to be doing on a building site, especially for those lads that do work. You could go sudden into a shed and there'd be some fucker tucked into a corner, sitting on an upturned bucket, smoking, and I never understood that, sure wouldn't it be boring him stupid to be doing that, and not going about working, or at least having a laugh with his mates. Because that's the great thing about the buildings, there's never any shortage of jokes, sure it's better than the telly betimes on the buildings. So little jobs like that. I was like the CIA, the secret service. Or I would be up on his roof, it was an acre of tiles up there, fixing leaks – or whatever he needed. Then, I don't know, he got himself into some tremendous bother, over-extended himself most like, and one morning when I came in, he was pacing about in the hall, this huge room with four marble statues, he told me who they were, Venus, Diana, and the others I forget, but, you know, very shapely girls those two were, and anyway, he says me to, 'Christy, there's no point coming in today, the sheriff will be up the drive in a minute, he's going to take everything away.' 'The sheriff?' I says, 'I didn't even know we had a sheriff in Portmarnock,' you know, thinking it made us sound like the wild west, as maybe we were really. 'Yes,' he says, 'himself and the bailiffs, you know, they're coming to take my bits and pieces, and the house is gone too, the bank has taken it back.' 'Jesus, boss,' says I. 'Yes,' he says, 'will you have a cup of coffee before you go?' Because one of the things I liked about working for him, was he had got me off the tea and on to the coffee. I still like drinking coffee, in his memory like. 'No,' I says, 'we can do better than that, you gather everything with the biggest value on it, boss, and stack it into the hall, and I'll bring round the van.' So I did, and we packed the Transit van with all these lovely pictures, I don't know if they were Rembrandts or whatnot, like your man stole from the house in the mountains, the General, but they probably were, and certain sticks of furniture he was keen on, Irish, he said, Irish tables, that's what the dealers like, and I suppose if we had had the time we might have prised out some of the marble fireplaces he had, which much to my surprise cost hundreds of thousands, because in the old days, demolishing houses, stuff like that would just go on the skip with everything else, but, you know, times had changed. But we worked as fast as we could, we had to leave poor Venus and Diana to the tender mercies of the bailiffs, we couldn't shift then on our own, but we stuffed the van, and then I got in the driver's seat, and he sat in beside me, wearing a pair of my old blue overalls, all paint marks and old patches of glue, and we set off down the avenue, and sure enough didn't the big bailiff's lorry pull in the gates just as we got halfway, and me pulling in on to the grass a bit to let them go by, with a friendly wave. Then we drove like maniacs out to the mountains, where his ould mother's house was, and he put all his loot into her garage, and then we drove off again, and I let him out at the Shelbourne Hotel, and I know he was raked over the coals in court after, and lost everything, but they didn't get that stuff we had hidden. And if you were asking me why I helped him with that, I would say to you, it was for the sake of fucking decency. It wasn't right that he was losing everything, the Bentley sports car in the garage, especially, not to mention probably Helga.

So when the guards came up the path, I was thinking naturally it was about that, as anyone would, and the blood drained from my arms, it's a terrible feeling, the feeling you are about to be nicked, but it wasn't about that at all, it was all about Peadar, and about how he had been found, and they had a suspect in custody in Galway, they'd be bringing him up to Dublin shortly, and they were very sorry, but they were obliged to tell me my son was dead, I don't think I ever spoke to such namby-pamby guards, and did I want to sit down, but sure I saved myself the trouble, and fell down in a faint in the corridor, and when I woke up I saw Christine's face hovering over me, and the tears running down her cheeks.

No one who has never lost a child can know what that feels like, let me tell you. Your child, even if he is walking around the world without you, is always somewhere inside you, I suppose he's your guts and innards really, and when you hear news like that, they might as well have opened you with a hacksaw, opened your chestbone I mean, and pulled everything out, because that's what it feels like. It's one of those feelings when you feel it you imagine you will never get over it, never recover, never want to be wandering down to boozer, you know, doing daily things. As a matter of fact all I could think of doing was holing up in the boozer, drinking, and Christine was home in the house, with the other poor childer, drinking her gin. That's how it was. Ugly long weeks of time then, and after they carved up poor Peadar and made their fucking notes, looked him all over to see what had murdered him, he was put into a box like an ould fella at the end of his days, and buried in Deansgrange. If I said to you I remember the occasion I would be lying, because I had two bottles of Powers in me, though I was standing straight for all that. They lowered him down, and somehow by the time of the hearing I was sober, and I sat in the court there in the Four Courts, and listened to those slimy fucking lawyers, and that's when the fury started.

By fuck I knew about PJ Sullivan, and where he lived, I
knew everything about him, it was in the *Evening Press*,
all the details, and anyhow, Peadar had spoken about him
to me before, as being his best pal and all the rest, though
I didn't like the fact that he was ten years older than him,
a man of twenty-seven, but I thought, well, sure that's
seminarians for you, or something along those lines. But
I was sure he was a wicked bad man, whatever his age,
and it came out in court what had happened, all the
details, how poor Peadar was fucking pushed off a cliff
when he was least expecting, I mean, the cunting
meanness of that, and when I heard that, I could feel the
poor boy falling, for fuck's sake, I sort of fell with him,
him bleeding like a pig, with wounds on his chest and
back from the rocks, like stab wounds if you were
stabbed with a lump hammer, like a fucking toothless
wolf had attacked him. And then this fucker PJ Sullivan,
fucking sobbing and crying, and then when he was
arrested, racing off before anyone could stop him, was he
trying to escape or what? And sure where did they think
he was going to run to on an island, and when he gets to
the cliffs at this spot called Dun Aengus, just above the
town apparently, and I would love to get out to the island
someday, to see where it all happened, not that I ever
will, doesn't he leg himself off those fucking cliffs, and
goes down into the sea, but sure, you couldn't drown a
cunt like that, the lifeboat was out already, after picking
up Peadar, and sure it picks him up, half-drowned I am
sure, but bobbing about like an eejit, probably all that
blubber keeping him afloat. Anyhows, this was the story,
no matter how the lawyers put it, and though he was
pleading guilty, they were looking for some what they
called *amelioration* of his sentence, because that was life,
right there, and just thirty years before it would have
been the gallows for him, my boys, but the judge pointed
out that it was a mandatory sentence, there could be no

fucking *amelioration*, no fucking anything but throw him
in the dungeon till the black heart rotted out of him, the
fucking killing murdering man, and I sat there in the
courtroom, oh, so polite they were, talking that legal
gobbledygook, and this fucking PJ sitting there, head
bowed, with his fucking accent from the other side of
Monkstown, his fecking mother in her nice coat, the
lovely hair-do, oh yes, even in her grief, her poor son, her
poor son, and the tears pouring out of her the whole
time, and him the savage really, dark-hearted killing
savage with his teeth drooling blood, so I gets up, when
all was done, when all was said and done, and went out
into Dublin, and walked with Christine along the river,
pelting with rain it was, we took no heed of it, the two of
us going along, the heads on us soaking, soaking, and
made my solemn resolutions, though I never breathed a
word to her.

She herself silent as the grave, walking along. These two
priests had given evidence. First thing was, they seen
these two fellas 'at it'. 'The perversion that most offended
God', the judge called it. Then they heard voices raised.
Shouting. They were going on about the voices raised
when Christine, she threw up, quietly, on to my folded
coat. Right there in the court.

PJ

So then it was all done and it was the life sentence for
me, and I was carried down the river and I suppose up
O'Connell Street in the van to Mountjoy, though I
couldn't see out the window, because there wasn't a
window, but for some reason I thought of all the people
of Dublin going about their business, schoolkids traipsing
home, mothers doing the shopping, layabouts begging off
foreigners and the like, and I thought, they are all angels
and saints, all of them, even those layabouts, heroic
dossers, I thought, living through their lives, moment to

moment, all accident really, nothing much planned, and if
planned, plans sundered and altered by accident, and
I wonder what was God's hand in it all, was this His
creation in the upshot, these souls going about from the
cradle to the grave, fulfilling their allotment of years, the
great gift of life as they say, and myself now sitting on an
iron bench, in an iron van, being brought away to my
fate in that dark old prison I had often passed, not even
registering it, like any other free man. And of course I was
to be a free man no longer, but I had seen the grief in his
father's face, I had, and I knew I had removed Peadar
from his own allotment of days, and I thought that was
indeed a ferocious crime, I was in agreement with the
judge, who called it 'an event beyond parallel in my time
on the bench'. And I was to go away now for good, like
a child sent out on a permanent holiday to his country
relatives, never to return, but not to experience the joys
of the country, reaching into old hayricks to find the
elusive eggs, being obliged to stay silent while my aunt
churned the butter, for fear of putting a *piseog* on it, and
silence so hard for a gossoon, and all the other magic of
the countryside, no, but the bleak dark room in that
ferocious solitude, peopled only by the lost, the screws
themselves sort of exiled from happiness in their way, and
the patronising chaplain with his hand on my hand, and
in a gesture like that you know you are doomed, and I
was never going to be priest now, no more than Peadar,
but a lost man, a Lifer, a devil. But none of it filled me
with fear as much as the sight of my mother, in the old
coat she always wore, and the neglected perm, terribly
thin now, still a young woman in her way, but her life
completely ruined. And I thought of the long days she
would spend in her house in Monkstown, and her husband
long dead, and the gramophone still glooming there,
losing its polish year by year, and the dust gathering on
everything she owned, layer after layer, and her withering,

withering, and the great wide bay glistening dark blue under the yellow moon as always, but she would never take comfort in that again, and she used to have this funny phrase she used, that something or other was as black as a giraffe's tongue, that was a saying she had, I never heard another person say it, and I don't even know if a giraffe's tongue is black, maybe it is, maybe a person could go into Dublin Zoo and have a look at the tongue of a giraffe, and verify it, but I knew from that day forth that her life, and the life of Peadar's people, would be as black as that, and blacker. And that I was the cause of it.

Christy

Mayhem. Anger. You can do anything with anger. I mean, the bit of the gospels that I really like, when PJ is reading to me, as he does sometimes in the night-times, is the time JC goes ape-shit over the moneylenders. Some of the holy bits go over my head, but that bit I understand. I understand it perfectly.

Otherwise I can't understand what got into me. But it got into me, whatever it was. Got into me with knobs on. Jesus. Like I say, I knew where PJ lived, of course I did. I mean, everything you hear at a trial, a trial like that, burns into your brain. You could be the fucking book of the trial, the judge could refer to you, to say out bits of it out again, sure you know it all, word for word. Burns into you. Longford Place, 13 Longford Place. Sure it's only back of Old Dunleary, where Christine was born. Old Dunleary was just a little fishing village onetime, then came the coalyard, then came the big houses on Longford Place. There's Longford Terrace as well, they're just gigantic fucking palaces. All the same, Longford Place, very nice houses. Very nice.

Very easy to break into too, if I say so myself. I'm thin

though, I can get into places other lads couldn't. I'm like Oliver Twist, in the film.

It was a very small window, into the scullery, there were big taps there for swilling out potatoes and carrots, handy for holding on to. When you go head first into a window, you want something below you to stop you breaking your neck. Try it, if you don't believe me. So I was in then, myself, alone, in the dark scullery, the house quiet as a tomb, all of Old Dunleary indeed, quiet, only now and then at intervals, no doubt decided by the Harbour Commissioners, the fog horn sounded in the bay. Long drawn out and mournful, like somebody had died. Or somebody was going to die. Like it was the banshee calling at the gable of a house.

So in through the kitchen I crept. It was a vaulted room, unusual. I saw a bottle of sour milk, I suppose for the bread PJ's mother would be making, I don't know why I noticed that. I had a sniff of it going by. It brought me back to my own mammy's house. She always had a bottle going sour. When you think of that. These days it's just the sliced pan and the Marietta biscuits. I opened the dresser drawer and chose a bread knife from the array of knives. She had everything you could wish, PJ's mother. It was a very pleasing room, that's all I can say, and that was only the kitchen. Up the narrow stairs I went stealthily. I had taken off my shoes in the scullery, they stood like two bent tin-scoops waiting for me. I was sort of frightened, even in my anger. I knew what I had to do, and I was fully intending to do it, with God's help, but I hoped I could keep my nerve now. I was trembling like a jelly. My legs felt weak. I wondered could I even lift the bread knife? So I raised it there on the stairs, just in case my arm failed me, and at least it would be already aloft. Kind of ridiculous, but the fear was only something wojus. So up I went like that, truly the very picture of a pantomime killer, I am sure. And I came through a glass door into the back hall, and moved along the corridor like a vengeful ghost, and into the lofty hallway. The stairs were as posh as a billiard hall, all mahogany, glistening, gleaming in the dark, though the street lights threw in a few bushels of brightness through the fanlight of the front door. Up up, I drove my feet, one after the other, in the old grey socks, builder's socks, that Christine had darned a hundred times, not the cleanest socks in Christendom by any means, but they carried me up. Then I was at a landing, full of pictures, of flowers, of far away places, I peered at one of them, it was that famous big church in Rome, and she had pictures of people I didn't know, how could I, maybe relatives, serious-looking people, staring at me as I passed. Oh, and I felt the true infidel and the intruder, of course I did. There were three doors on the landing and I opened each one gingerly, one after the other, not making a sound, the hinges good and oiled, and peered into each room, but it was just a sitting room and two little bedrooms, and nothing in them stirring. So one more flight for my sins, the knife still raised, ridiculous, till I reached the top landing, and now I could hear something, the sound of a human being, moving about maybe. I was horror struck suddenly, as if I was the one in danger. I was so frightened the piss ran down my leg. It was three in the morning and these sounds of movement were unexpected. All the same I moved patiently forward, intent, gliding really, and I put my free hand on the doorknob of the middle door, it was fancier than the others and nicely carved, I always had an eye for good carpentry, and I pushed forward into the slightly different darkness, it was dark but the street lights were there again, and suddenly I could see her, PJ's mother, in her nightie, walking across the room, as if to welcome me, I don't know why, but she probably didn't even see me, I saw a big bed against the wall, the room smelled of something, camphor or something, perfume or something, and before she could really know what was happening, but just in the moment she saw me, I struck. God forgive me, it was like hitting a little bird. It was all so sudden and savage, I could hardly credit it myself. I felt like a wolf. I thought there'd be some resistance, some difficulty, so I put all my weight into it. But the knife seemed to go right through her, as if she wasn't really there. And she folded on to the floor like a headscarf, like someone dropped a headscarf. There was nothing else to it. I fled away, bathed in horror. It was Vincent Price in *The House of Wax*. Holy and merciful God.

For two years no one knew who done it. Then I told Christine. I was like a poisoned rat, the guilt of it was poisoning me, so I told her. She just stared and stared at me, completely unable to understand. She didn't even say, 'Why did you do it?' She didn't even say that. 'What about Doreen and Mickey?' was what she said. 'What are they, ghosts as well?' What did she mean? She went straight to the guards, she wasn't having that. My own wife, and I do not blame her. She was right, dead right. It was Mr Herman Good of Dawson Street defended me, but you know, there was no defence. I had done it, that was it. I done it because PJ killed my son, and I killed his mother because that seemed to me like for like. It took a great effort. An eye for an eye, and a tooth for a tooth. Something that was precious to him, for something that was precious to me.

PJ

I remember sitting in here, with all that going on outside. My cellmate in those days was a Russian lad, Vlad, who was supposed to have killed two men in a fight in Burdock's chipper, not that he admitted to it. 'I ham hinnocent,' he would say. 'Hinnocent, Patrick, as God is my vitness.' And, maybe he was, you could never tell, only, his trial had said different. But he was here in those days, occupying Christy's bed. And I couldn't have had a better pal. OK, he was a rough man, from the forests outside Moscow, where, he said, the sun bouncing off the snow would burn you and blind you, in the freezing cold of winter, and there were wolves and boars still where he lived, that would take you off a forest path if you let them, and devour you at their leisure. The screw on this landing was a man called McAllister, a big burly man, he was probably a Protestant with a name like that, but that was neither here nor there, and he wasn't a nice man. Oh, he was anxious for me to have all the latest details of the trial. How the killer had crept in and murdered my mother in her bath, this is what he told me, and as he spoke I could imagine a shadowy man creeping through the rooms of our old house, maybe hearing a little noise in the bathroom, and finding her all convenient in the bath. I couldn't get my head around all that, though I was a murderer myself. And to think of her, a person of absolute modesty, meeting her end in that fashion. And he would go out then, all delighted with himself, and why he had it in for me quite so badly, I don't know, only he said he didn't like queers and homos, I mean, he might have been telling me the same things, you know, but with a kind and considerate voice, since we weren't allowed newspapers, but no, it was all to terrorise me, and when he was gone again Vlad would come closer to me, and put his hand on my shoulder, and say, 'Not vorry, Patrick, this man is bad cunt.'

Years later they let Vlad go free. New evidence had come to light, he had been innocent all along. I missed that Russian bear. And one day the cell door opens, it's McAllister, with another man, I hadn't an idea who he was, never saw him in my life. 'Here's your new cellmate,' says McAllister. And I suddenly felt gratitude to him for putting someone in with me. In comes the fellow, a skinny streak of a chap about ten years older than myself, a wiry bouncy man, humorous looking, I liked him instantly, he strides in confidently and throws his few things on Vlad's old bed, and nods to me, and we introduce ourselves, as innocent as you like. 'Howaya,' he says. 'The name's Christy, Christy Dwyer.' 'Hello,' I says, 'PJ, PJ Sullivan.' And we're standing there like that, we were shaking hands, like the good old lags we were, and he was nodding then, and then his head began nodding a bit faster, like he was thinking, and then into my brain came rushing the thought, like a hare bounding, like a hare running fast, Christy Dwyer, this couldn't be the man that killed my mother? They'd never put us in together, sure there'd be murder. Christy Dwyer, Christy Dwyer. Well, I supposed it might be a common name enough. And we sorted the room out between us, as you do, and he had a little packet of nude pictures he had brought in from his other cell, wherever it had been, and he asked me was it alright if he put them on the wall beside his bed, he had the bit of blue tack. And I wondered why was he asking me, was it at the back of his mind that I might be a priest? Did he suspect also, if only subconsciously? Did he already know? And I said I didn't mind at all, not a bit, it would brighten the place up. So he laboriously arranged them on the wall, and he told me their names, like he knew them all, like they were friends of his. But they were just the girls off a newspaper. And he had his little radio, with the Sellotape over it, and he said he liked Ronan Collins, he liked to listen to Ronan Collins, because it calmed his nerves. He said he suffered a bit from his nerves. And then, I don't know how, suddenly out of blue, he rushes at me. It was like being assaulted by a huge metal spring. 'Are you the fucker killed my son?' he said, and gave me a little push, like he wanted to give space to confess, and I drew back then, like a villain in an old western. If we'd had six guns we'd have drawn them, but all we had was our sorrow, and he leaped at my throat, by God I could hear McAllister laughing like a crazy man behind the cell door, with the little bracket open, laughing, peering in, what a great lark, Christy at my throat, I fought back as best I could, *this is the man who murdered my mother*, and we went at each other, oh hammer and tongs, I tried to beat him with my fists, but I'm a terrible fighter, if there'd been a chair in the cell I could have tried to smash his head with it, just to stop him, he was like a force of nature, then he punched me clear across the room, a little man like that, he had a ferocious punch, I staggered against the crapper, he leaped on top of me and tried to force my head in, 'I'll fucking drown you, you cunt!' he shouted, I managed to heave him off me, I was absolutely terrified now, I knew he was going to kill me if he could, he was going to fight me till he killed me, wear me down and kill me, he was wiry and astonishingly strong. But he didn't have my weight, and he broke away from me, and leapt to the bunk, trying to tear the ladder from it, so he could beat me to death with it, I supposed, and I rushed across the room at him, like a bloody rhino, and tried to crush him against the metal bed. I heard McAllister then rattling the key, and in he rushed, and to tell you the truth there was a terrible concerned look on his face now, like he knew it had gone too far, and he would get the blame, and he dragged us apart, not laughing now, because he realised we would both be happy to murder each other, there was a fury in us both, myself too now, the whole thing had pressed the fury button in me, a tremendous thing built up like a volcano, we would have been glad to see blood and hear bones breaking, and McAllister was caterwauling now, screaming at us to stop, and in rushed one of the other screws, Bennett I think it was, and he didn't seem to think it was a good joke either, to put the two of us in the one cell together, without due notice, but suddenly,

suddenly I was exhausted, and Christy too, he was so
tired he was mewling like a cat, and they got us apart,
pushed us down to the floor, like the afternoon wrestlers
that used to be on UTV, the rage in us gone now and the
superhuman strength that goes with it, and they put
the bracelets on us, our hands behind our backs, and
seeing we were quiet now, bollixed as Christy might say,
McAllister went out and phoned the prison doctor, and
he came and injected us, like we were wild animals being
caught for the zoo. And sleep came upon me like a
lorryload of darkness tipped over my head.

In the small hours when I woke, groggily, I could just make
out Christy in the darkness. They had left us together,
after all. The light from the prison yard shone in the little
window, and lay in a glistening bar across his face. I
looked at him. He was covered in bruises from the fight.
There was a little blood on his bald head, whether his or
mine I couldn't know. I looked at his face for a long time,
him still sleeping. I suddenly knew something, it was a
moment of simple compassion, and in that moment
I realised it had been a long time since I had considered
another man's pain. I mean, considered it with the
piercing sympathy of an ordinary priest. I was looking
at the face of a suffering man. And in that face I saw a
shadow of the face I had loved best in the world. And
suddenly the worst thing was not that he had murdered
my mother, but that I had killed his son. How can I truly
describe that moment? I feel it might be important to do
so. But I haven't got the words for it.

I didn't have much time to think about it either, because
twenty minutes later I began to feel very strange. It was
the blood had gone cold in my brain, if there is blood in
a brain, I suppose there must be, and the strangest feeling
came over me, like there was poison in my throat, or my
throat was being throttled by invisible hands. A horrible

dreepy sensation in my chest, extremely unpleasant and alarming. And then I was thinking, well, if this is going to carry me off, good riddance to bad rubbish, and then, thinking better of this maybe, I called out to the sleeping form of Christy. Or I meant to call out, but the sound that came was just a meagre whisper. I whispered and whispered, meagrely. I suddenly knew my life depended on waking this man. But my throat seemed closed, and you can't get a note from a flute that's stoppered up. Nevertheless I strained to do so. Then Christy Dwyer seemed to come awake of his own accord. 'Mercy of good Jesus,' he said. 'I thought I was dead.' Then I push on with my whispers. 'What are you saying there, bud?' he said, like we were men meeting at a bus stop. 'I can't fucking hear you.' Then he bounced himself closer to me, he had to edge really close, and get his ear right to my mouth. I asked him to shout for McAllister. 'I will, I will,' he says, 'no bother.' Which is just how Christy is, helpful by nature. Despite everything. 'No panic,' he says, 'that's the main thing.' Then he caterwauls for McAllister or Bennett, some bloody screw to come running. As it was late in the evening, it was a lad called Doyle was on, one of the decenter screws, to be fair, and Christy said I was pegging out, as he called it, and someone better get me to the doc. So Doyle goes out and fetches another night man from the tier below, and they bring in an ancient wheelchair that they must keep somewhere, and I'm heaved up into it, still with the blasted bracelets on, and then I'm being wheeled out. And then it was down to the yards by the old service stairs, Doyle and the other lad helping me down, the wheelchair going bang bang bang, you'd think there might be a lift in Mountjoy, except it was built in the eighteen-hundreds, and Christy's voice in the distance now, shouting 'Can't you take these fucking handcuffs off me before you go?'

Christy

Triple bypass, Mercer's Hospital, armed guard on the
ward door, so they tell me, for fuck's sake. In those days
PJ was still a young fella, really. I drank a bottle of
whiskey every day for ten years, never took a feather out
of me. Soft, these lads, from the wrong side of
Monkstown.

So what happens next, McAllister, who was supposed to
be just the cunt in this story, goes all Mother Teresa on
me. Thinks he done me wrong and what's more thinks
he done PJ wrong but worser. Wants to make it good.
Seemingly he goes over to PJ the few times bringing him
fucking grapes and Lucozade. PJ, being a confused sort
of bollocks, is worried about me and sends me a message
that he bears no grudge. Then McAllister, in this bid to
become the fucking Gandhi of Mountjoy, wants to know
what I think of that. I says PJ can fuck off with himself
and his worry and I don't care if he dies. But I must of
said it a shade nicely or something because back comes
the message that he's glad I'm OK and when he's all
healed he wants to come back to the cell. You put him
anywhere near me, I says to McAllister, and I'll gut him
with a spoon. Well, says McAllister, I'm glad you can let
bygones be bygones. Eh, what, I says, what the what?
I'm looking at him. You couldn't make it up.

So after a couple of months, they bring him back in to
me. Well I had nearly forgotten he existed, you know the
way you sort of do, forget everything, in here, including
yourself. Ah yes but the real reason for McAllister's Holy-
Joe toing-and-froing in *my* opinion was McAllister was
terrified this whole thing would get out, go beyond our
floor, it would come out, in the papers even, what he
done, putting us two together for the pure divilment of it,
and he was close to retirement, wasn't he, just a few
years, and he didn't want to be getting the sack, and

losing his pension, so he sorta *plots* to have PJ brought back. That's my best guess anyhow, call me cynical if you like, and anyhow one day, the door opens, and the fucker's back, still in the wheelchair, looking somewhat better for his holiday. 'How are ya, ya poor cunt?' I says, you know the way you would. But he was very tired from the transfer, and all he could do was climb into the lower bed, sure I was happy enough to swap, took down Samantha and Co, and transferred myself and themselves to the upper regions. And McAllister was in fussing, and the doc too, he must have been in the same stew of worry, the bad-hearted bastard, sticking that needle in us, I hardly think he had the go-ahead for that. Although, alright, when you're feeling poorly, he does come, promptly enough. But one word from me, or one word from PJ, just then, well, fuck, they were both for the fucking high jump, no doubt about it. So we were suddenly in a state of, I don't know, not exactly the upper hand, hardly, like, we weren't in the driving seat, no sir, but we had a little bit on those fuckers, and that's very useful in here, that's better than fucking money.

I mean, influence, but not with the real people. I mean, screws are nearly like prisoners, in a funny sort of way. The real people, the real fucking people, are the fuckers sit on the parole board. And then the fucking minister of the day, peering at your crime on some bit of paper put under his nose, like it was a bit of dog dirt on his dinner plate. I don't know, every seven years they have a little think about you. Will we, won't we, let this fucker free? In my case, won't, with knobs on.

PJ

I was as sick as a dog for months. Then slowly slowly I was getting better, I could feel the body picking up, but I hadn't the slightest bit of energy. Suddenly, when I was put back into my cell, it was all down to Christy to keep

49

me going, which is ridiculous, when you think about it. I mean, even natural justice would say, he was hardly the man for the job. But he didn't seem to think so. Now, he is a very strange man. He has the most extraordinary anger in him. Sometimes he berates me – for instance, for my ignorance of football. But we never played football at school, we weren't allowed. But he worships Liverpool, he has worshipped them all his life. One time he was trying to find out the outcome of a match, he calling out the window to a mate of his on Tier Four, it was a Derby match, between Liverpool and Everton, and I asked him where Everton was. 'You're a stupid cunt,' he said, with sudden and absolute viciousness. 'Have you never heard of Goodison Park?' 'I was just asking where it was, Christy, you don't have to lose your rag.' 'It's in fucking Liverpool, you stupid fucking cunt.' 'Christy, Christy, just take it easy.' Then I said nothing for a bit, and I said, maybe in truth to tease him, 'Liverpool is in Liverpool, and Everton is in Liverpool, so why are they enemies?' I said, 'What's wrong with you, what's fucking wrong with you?' he cries, like a man in pain. 'I don't want to be locked up with a fucker doesn't know fuck, doesn't know where anything is, doesn't know Everton are the devil's spawn . . .' This he roared out. Then he turns to the window, in full flower of rage. 'And you won't even tell me the fucking score!' And he was steaming now, boiling with rage, and outrage, and disgust.

But it was just things like that he got mad about. Otherwise, for a man that had killed, he was very easy-going. I mean, we're talking bed baths here, bed baths. And things like the past, he was very different about. He was very diffident about the past, and what he had done, even what I had done. Otherwise we wouldn't have had a chance. The first thing was his looking after me. Now, no nurse could have gone to more trouble. I know this sounds ridiculous too. This murderer, this man who had

killed the mother of the man who had killed his son,
almost mothering that man. Almost fathering. And weak
as I was in those days, and I still get dickie days I must
confess, something came back to me from the great fog
that lay over my memories of Peadar. I say a great fog,
because something was happening to those memories,
something I didn't want, they were fading and twisting.
I knew I still loved him, I knew I still adored him, and
I still didn't know why I had killed him. I just didn't have
an understanding of it. I still don't. I used to try and
remember things Peadar had said, just ordinary things,
about antiquities, about his feeling for Jesus Christ,
which was very strong, about growing up in Monkstown
Farm, and the story about his grandfather killed at the
gate by who was it? Yes, Con Daly, and he often told me
about his own father, and the times they had going about
together, I used to be very surprised, because I thought,
I don't know why, but I thought an old-fashioned man
like his father wouldn't accept him, but apparently he
did, he really did, and when he was little they used to go
into town together, Peadar told me this, and they'd trot
along to the Natural History Museum in Merrion Square,
because his father loved the exhibits, the Irish Elk that
was extinct in Ireland, and the jars of specimens, and
Peadar kind of enjoyed them too, and on Fridays
Christy'd walk him over Dunedin Field to the dance hall
when he was bigger, because a lad like Peadar could be
murdered on Dunedin Field, even though he was from
that side of Monkstown himself, there was a tree there in
the centre of the field where a gay man had been hanged,
as a matter of fact, now I think of it, there was a terrible
hatred of what they called queers, and they knew Peadar
was one of them, and there were lads would have gladly
beaten him to a pulp, but his father, yes, Christy Dwyer,
the very same, who in everyone's eyes was a manly sort
of man, I suppose the phrase might be, well, they'd never

go near Peadar while Christy was with him. Because
Peadar loved to dance, Christy would bring him over to
the hall, and then smoke fags outside in the June dark,
waiting for him. And Peadar told me things like that.
And, because I was afraid I'd forget that too, I said it
to Christy one night. It was probably as much as two
years in, because truth to tell we were both afraid to
broach certain subjects, for fear of further mayhem. I
said, 'Christy, I don't know if I ever told you, but Peadar
really really loved you. He thought the world of you, as
a matter of fact.' Christy looks at me, like it was the last
thing he had expected me to say, the last thing on earth
he had expected to hear, from anyone. He had been
telling me about the intricacies of the football pools just
moments before. I had surprised him. And he said
nothing in reply. But I could see he was affected by it.
'And I just want to say, and I said it at my trial, I am
sorry for what happened. I am sorry for what I did.' Still
he said nothing. I was going to try again, and began to
say something else, but he stopped me, 'It's alright,' he
said, 'I fucking know. I fucking know. I know you're
fucking sorry.' He was quiet again then for a moment.
'I know it. Because I'm fucking sorry, I am so fucking
completely fucking sorry for what I did to your ma.'
Then the cell was vibrating, it's the only word for it.
At the risk of sounding hyper-religious, it did come into
my mind that something pretty serious was happening,
something I thought that Jesus Christ Himself might
know about. He was after all a man who had nothing
too. Christy was trembling anyhow, and he was as open
as a book, wide open, I might have said anything to him,
and there was a question I had been longing to ask him,
but never could, because it sounded like an accusation,
but it wasn't an accusation. This matter had haunted me,
and sometimes in the dark of the night it used to make
me so angry, and it would take a hundred paternosters

to feel even half-calm again, and not want that instant, that very instant, to murder Christy in the bunk above. He was standing there, like a target, with the gentleness available only to the wolf. So I thought this was the moment to ask him. 'Can I just ask you one thing about that, Christy, if you don't mind?' I said. I knew I was instantly on dangerous ground, killing ground. 'What,' he said. And he didn't sound exactly friendly. 'Why did you have to kill her in her bath?' I said. There was a long, long silence. He wasn't looking at me now, he was looking at the floor. He swallowed. He swallowed like a boa constrictor, whether to pull something further in, or eject it, I didn't know. 'I didn't,' he said then, simply, in a quiet voice, as if in all honesty he expected to be believed, it was very impressive, it was the voice of a man praying in private. 'As God is my witness. I didn't kill her in her bath. It was in the bedroom. Which is bad enough.' 'Well,' I said, 'if that's true, to tell you the truth that makes an enormous difference to me.' 'Well, it is true,' he said. 'Not that I couldn't lie to you, I could. I'd fucking lie to any man if I thought it would get me out of trouble. Who told you it was in the bath?' 'McAllister, years ago.' 'Well, now, McAllister,' says Christy, and left it at that, as if he need say nothing further.

That kept me going for a long time. You might ask why it would, but it did. It was somehow easier then to slop out with Christy, look forward to the three square meals, be talking and sleeping and farting, Christy nattering away as is his wont – all the history of nothing that passes for life here. Little by little all I could see was a man, another man like myself in this lost world, and though I hated him too now and then, and he me, and that hatred would burn between us betimes, slowly slowly the hatred abated, and we lived together here, old enemies that have reached an accommodation, out of necessity but also by strange choice. We were souls at least burned in the same fire.

And that is a great mystery to me, and remains so. As if, having done the worst thing to each other, we could do no further harm, or any, really. And there was safety in that. Like the old world of my childhood. And, in this strange atmosphere, the shades of Peadar and my mother were somehow given a sort of life. A sort of permanent presence. Inside this peculiar mechanism, this whirring projector, this engine of Christy and me. Floating here, between us. And loved, fiercely loved. I barely know what I am saying. I am trying to unlock a riddle. Yes, we were wary of each other for a long time after, Christy and me. But we made peace with each other. How that came about is a long long story, a story about nothing, of meaningless words, two prisoners together, getting through the day, eating our grub, like I say, waiting for letters that never came, pissing in the toilet, slowly telling our stories to each other, as if we were the first people in the world, the only people, and the last people, two aging *bastards* in a ten-by-ten in the Joy. And we knew we were nothing, we knew we were forgotten men, who would never have business again in the world, who would never again walk about the streets of the city, in the manner of the living. And I think it took a long long time for me to *realise*. Not that I had *loved* Peadar, which I did, with all my heart and soul, but that I had *killed* him. I mean, you'd think that would be the first realisation, but in effect it has been the last. Truly, really, understand what I had done. The actual act of pushing him off the cliff, for a reason I knew not why. Then, having accounted myself at last a bona-fide murderer, other things hit me with a new force. That my mother was gone now and there wasn't a soul in the world knew or cared where I was, and rightly so. The country uncles probably all dead, and so on. Alone. Not crying alone, I mean, not upset alone, feeling sorry for myself, no, not really, though in here sometimes you do feel a bit sorry for yourself, stupidly,

but – lonesome. Like a petrol pump once I saw in a little
Wicklow village, passing through in a van of seminarians,
on our way to swim at Arklow, one of the very first pumps,
I'll be bound, ancient now, rusty, not used for a decade,
the garage itself long gone, just the rusty petrol pump, on
its own, useless, doing nothing. Like me. And my next
thought was, time to go. Finish off what I tried to do at
Dun Aengus, all those years ago, as Christy rightly said.

A moment.

I had a thought once I might go out to the missions, learn
Swahili in Kenya, or the Congo, something like that,
make myself useful there.

But – Peadar lost everything.

Christy

Now we've lived together in contentment, more or less,
for nigh on twenty year. Like turtle doves. – In prison,
I mean, for fuck's sake, the chances of that.

A few years ago when my case came up again, word
came back that they were going to keep me here for the
rest of my life, as they called it. What fucking life. And
this was after saying a few years before that, that I was
going to serve thirty years minimum. I mean, how nice
was that? Very fucking unfriendly. Then, lo and behold,
PJ is reviewed, and suddenly it's, yes, he can be released,
November coming, whatever, and all the official lingo.
Jesus, Jesus. And PJ starting down at the notice, like he
was going to be hanged. And me fucking panicking,
thinking, holy God, do I have to sit in there with some
other fucker for the rest of my born days? I mean, I was
so upset I threw up my dinner. Right there on the cell
floor. Fucking hamburger without the bun, I mean I ask
you, and I don't remember eating carrots, but there's
always carrots in puke. They must be inner carrots that

come up in an emergency.

But and anyway.

And I suddenly realised, I suddenly realised, what I owed to McAllister.

That fucker McAllister, yes indeed, he seemed to get a great kick out of us, before he retired. Professional fulfilment, he called it. That he'd thrun us in together but we hadn't killed each other. He just couldn't get over it. Restored his faith in humanity, he said. Nearly got him sacked, more like. Lying fucker. But no, he said, no, it was a miracle. He was glad he'd done it. But, he was a fucker, all the same. He was always saying, 'Now, Dwyer, don't turn your back on your man, he's a shirt-lifter.' On and on with that. Till the day came and I said, 'Listen, Mr McAllister, you say that once more, once more, I'm going to steal a long knife out of the kitchens, hone it to the thickness of a nail, and drive it into your skull. Just so you know.' Now, McAllister knew I probably wouldn't do that, but still, it was me saying it, wasn't it? That had done terrible deeds. So he shuts up with his homo remarks. Now, don't get me wrong. One time, years ago, when I was a married man, I used to get these videos off of a fellow in the People's Park in Dunleary, and one time he throws a few into a bag, as usual, and I bring them home. Christine was out at the bingo, so 'Bingo for me,' says I, and puts on the first tape – by Jesus, it was these fellas going at each other. I mean, they were going. Holy God. So I pull out the tape and bring it back and give the man a box on the ear for himself. But, you know, that's just me. PJ might have enjoyed that tape, I don't know. It's just I didn't. But it doesn't mean I think it's unnatural. I just think I don't want to be doing it.

I like PJ. Anyone would.

But howandever, without McAllister, I'd a' been alone

in here. Even with some other cellmate, I'd a' been alone. That's how I see it anyhow.

Look, you're probably asking yourself, why are they telling us their story? Well, the truth is, we have this plan, you see. Yes, our little plan, we call it. When it comes up in conversation, as it does a lot, that's how we refer to it. So, before we carry out our plan – call it our escape plan, if you like – we wanted to tell our side of things, even if our side of things isn't that . . . flattering. But you know, in the papers, the *Herald* or the *Press* as may be, we're only called killers, perverts, and all the rest, with demon eyes and vile and evil hearts. But yes, we are murderers, we must be, that's why we're here. But PJ says, PJ says, God is in rage just as much as love. He says to me, 'Christy, did you never read the Old Testament?' 'Old testicles,' I says. 'No,' he says, 'it's still the Bible. It's still the holy book. There's a lot of human rage in the Old Testament. Just fucking saying,' says he. – No, well, he never says fuck, does he? You know, because you've been listening to him.

The plan. And my next thought right anenst the word 'plan' is: Christine. Let me tell you the little story of Christine. It's the story of Christine, Doreen and Mickey, as a matter of fact. Talk about triple bypass. As soon as I fessed up about PJ's ma, it was all over. For her. For me, it was going on as before, to tell you the truth. Look it, well I know it, I am a very sentimental man. There's some things that make my cry, in a foolish sort of way. I mean, I like Charlie Landsborough. I think that says it all. But there's another thing that lives on a tier above foolishly weeping, and that's the feeling I have for Christine. I knew well my luck when I had her, and I know well my misfortune in losing her. A woman is a world, isn't she? She's a country, with airports and cities, she's a sort of district where a man can live. And only there. Yes, I will admit that, for the last fifteen years and more, I was hoping she would come and see me. You know, the families gather at the old high gates at visiting time, and I am sure that's a strange sight to people passing up the canal to the Glasnevin Road. Maybe they pity them, maybe they find them disgusting. But what are they, only fucking angels, the families, the brothers and sisters, the mothers and fathers, that have kept faith with their relative. Criminal relative now, as may be. But kept faith. And want to see them, want to sit at the fucking plastic tables and have a natter, about nothing and everything, praying, praying Johnnie is still off the drugs, and hasn't been fucking raped by some madman, and so on, and so forth.

God forbid.

Which reminds me. The other Big Thing that happened in our time together. Me, I was stuck in here with a terrible ould head cold. PJ was obliged to go walking about the yard on his ownio. His constitutional, he calls it. Three fucking bad lads lay into him. Now, that's unusual enough, you might be surprised to hear. There's mostly young lads in here. It's like a college, they come in for a few years, and then they go. Of course, a lot of them come in again – 'to do their masters', as PJ calls it. But they're mostly quiet lads, druggies and the like, thieves. But these three fellas were murderous cunts, didn't like PJ, didn't like his crime, thought they could improve on the decisions of the penal system. Beat him black and blue, broke the right side of his jaw, broke an arm, nearly burst the stomach out of him, he was another month in hospital, and when he came back he looked like jack. Poor bollocks. And, he never once complained about it. Didn't want revenge, doesn't believe in it, so I tore the leg off the table we had then, stuck it into my trouser leg like Long John Silver, and went down into the yard to look for the three fellas. But, they'd been transferred to

Portlaoise. Lucky for them! Jesus. I was mashing up
his grub for months. Baby food, army hash, like when
Peadar was a baby. 'Will you mash that for me, Christy?'
Christine would say.

But she has never come. My informant on Tier Two, who
knows everything about what happens in the outside
world, how he knows I couldn't say, but I have a little
suspicion there's a mobile phone involved, but however
he knows, he keeps me updated about Doreen, who
married an ESB man, one of those lads who go out after
a storm and get your electric back for you, up on the
lampposts. You know? And Mickey's gone to England,
just like his da, but he's import-export, whatever that is.
Import-export. Sounds fancy. But they've never come to
visit neither. I wrote to Christine three hundred thousand
times, asking for to see her, and how very very fucking
sorry I was, and I wrote to my son and daughter, but, I
suppose they have made a clean break. And I understand
all that. I don't blame them. And I would really love to see
them again, but I won't, I know that now. Stupid fucking
Christy Dwyer, took twenty years to get the fucking
message. Dense fucker.

Maybe if we meet again in heaven, all – what do you call
it? – earthly things'll have passed away, and we'll be
hunky-dory again. I hope so.

Fed up with it. Lovely and all as living with PJ is, well,
it's not really a life, is it? It's funny that we both reached
the same moment, at the same time – the moment of
being completely fucking fed completely up with this
fucking how's-your-father.

You can understand that.

No, no, I'm not really telling the fucking truth here. The
truth is very fucking simple. PJ doesn't want to get out,
and I don't want to stay here without him.

Two sorts of sweat. Him sweating at the thought of freedom, at the fucking fearful thought of freedom, 'Blueberry Hill' how are you, and me, well, me, I never expected freedom, not this long time, no, I know what the minister said about me in the papers, never a crime so heinous, that's the word he chose, never a crime so heinous, killing an old lady, as bad as killing a garda, and once he said that . . . But I'm not going to sit in here without PJ. Jesus, I suppose it was all plain as day to him, when he told me about his release. And him looking at my face. White as a peeled banana. And he says, 'What's wrong, Christy?' and sure fuck it, I threw up, and then I burst into tears, didn't I, like a foolish child, and PJ is on is knees trying to mop up the puke, and me crying, and then he fucking forgets about the puke, and yes, and alright, he comes over to me, and he puts an arm around my shoulder, and he says, 'This won't do, Christy,' he says, I mean, was that homo or what, yes, and I don't fucking care if it was, I fucking love that fucking man, that fucking fucker PJ, and I'm gabbling and crying, and he says, 'Look it, Christy, we have to have a plan.' Formulate a plan, was the way he put it, actually. And he never says 'look it', I was only adding on a bit there.

'But PJ,' says I, 'I'm fucking happy for you, ha? At least one of us is getting out. You'll have a grand old time. Walking up O'Connell Street as happy as a lark, and going into Devito's Amusements, all sorts of crack.'

Oh, but, the ghastly white face on him then too, like I had just described hell.

'I don't fucking think so, Christy,' he says, maybe one of only two or three times I ever heard him curse. 'They'll crucify me, Christy. They'll have my guts for garters. And proper order.'

Then him shivering, shivering, like a mangey cat.

Then the weeping again. Weeping, weeping. Like the

waterfall in Powerscourt. The first time in thirty years I really cried. So that will tell you.

Anyway, our plan. We've been hatching a plan. There's been a lot of planning to the plan, you might say. Now, look it, the fags might carry me off, I'm sixty-nine years old for the love of Mike, PJ has the dickey heart, but well, no, we could be hanging on for another twenty years, me in here and him outside, knowing our luck. So we were thinking, how's about a little pact. We smuggle in two big knives from the kitchens – it was threatening to stab McAllister put that in my mind – then we set ourselves up here, on the floor here, face to face, and we'll, you know, hold the knives good, and PJ will aim for my heart, and I'll aim for his. Not in sorrow or anger, but in a friendly way. Because, make no mistake, we are great mates. And just in case we turn out not to be in the last analysis, as the fella said, we're going to swear on PJ's Bible not to be jammy fuckers. Then, at a signal of our choice, we'll strike in the same instance, and we've sworn on his ould bible, Old Testament and all, as I just said, that neither of us will draw back at the last minute, and if one of us is going to do that, we'll say so, scout's honour, and call it off. Because otherwise one of us will end up on a second charge of murder, for fuck's sake. And it'll be just the same thing all over again. So then we'll be sure to strike deep, make sure we get through the ribs and touch the heart, because that's how you do it, it'd be easier with a gun, but on the other hand it's very hard to fire two guns at the exact same time. With the knives we'll have some leeway. If one blade is turned by a rib, we can give it another bash, you know, that sort of thing. Anyway that's our plan, that's what's going to happen next, but we don't expect you to want to be here to see it, so it'll be after. And then, you see, it won't be suicide at all, and we can both skip Limbo, which PJ tells me is a pain in the hole. Though he didn't put it that way.

And if it's going to be Hell or Heaven for us, we'll let the Big Man decide. If it's going to be Hell, better if we go together anyhow, since we're used to each other now. Because, the time comes when you hear the signal, and it's time to be going. Life is sweet, of course it is, even in here. There are moments. Good moments, strange to relate. When everything is still, for instance, and you're just lying on your bunk, with Samantha Fox and Linda Lusardi for company on the wall, and PJ below, and a nice fag for yourself, glowing like a glow worm in the darkness, and the whole prison as may be is sleeping, all the weary souls, the young lads and the middle-aged men and the old, sleeping, dreaming their dreams, the murderers and the thieves, under the old washbasin of starlight, here in our mansion beside the Royal Canal. But the hour comes when you seem to hear the bell, and the owner of the boat is calling. 'Come in, PJ Sullivan, come in, Christy Dwyer.'

Our plan, you see. That's what's going to happen next.

He assumes the position of Fats Domino, as if at the piano, a little crouched, his body swung sideways, looking out, smiling broadly, head tilted back, and pretending to play the notes. He sings the first verse of 'Blueberry Hill':

'I found my freedom . . .' (*etc.*)

Now the piano starts to come in faintly, then clearer, then louder. PJ starts to dance a seventies dance with some aplomb.

He sings the second verse.

Then full band, tremendously. PJ really quite a good dancer.

The third and fourth verses.

Music fades, PJ and Christy look at each other, laughing, really laughing.

Almost hysterical with laughter, they hold on to each other. Suddenly no sound, just them together in a fast embrace.

Dark.

End.